Profiles of the Presidents

ANDREW JOHNSON

★ ★ ★

Profiles of the Presidents

ANDREW JOHNSON

by Michael Burgan

Content Advisers: Kendra A. Hinkle and Jim Small, Historians, Andrew Johnson National Historic Site, Greeneville, Tennessee

Reading Adviser: Dr. Linda D. Labbo, Department of Reading Education, College of Education, The University of Georgia

Compass Point Books
3109 West 50th Street, #115
Minneapolis, MN 55410

Visit Compass Point Books on the Internet at *www.compasspointbooks.com*
or e-mail your request to *custserv@compasspointbooks.com*

Photographs ©: White House Collection, Courtesy White House Historical Association, cover, 1;
Hulton/Archive by Getty Images, 6, 7, 8 (bottom), 9, 13, 18, 21, 25, 26, 32, 36 (all), 37, 38, 41, 42, 47,
49 (top), 50, 54 (top right), 56 (bottom left & right), 59 (left, all); North Wind Picture Archives, 8 (top),
12 (bottom), 14, 20, 23, 24, 31 (all), 33, 35, 40, 43, 57 (left), 58 (left); Courtesy of Capital Area
Preservation, Inc., Raleigh, North Carolina, 10; Bettmann/Corbis, 11, 30; Lombard Antiquarian Maps
& Prints, 12 (top), 54 (left); Courtesy Andrew Johnson National Historic Site, Greenville, TN, 15; G.E.
Kidder Smith/Corbis, 17, 55 (left); Stock Montage, 22, 39; Library of Congress, 27, 49 (bottom), 56
(top right); Corbis, 28, 45; Tennessee State Museum, Tennessee Historical Society Collection, 46;
Courtesy of HarpWeek, LLC, 48; Department of Rare Books and Special Collections, University of
Rochester Library, 54 (bottom right); Texas Library & Archives Commission, 55 (top right); Bruce
Burkhardt/Corbis, 55 (bottom right); Courtesy of the South Dakota State Historical Society-State
Archives, 57 (right); Union Pacific Historical Collection, 58 (right); Denver Public Library, Western
History Collection, 59 (right).

Editors: E. Russell Primm, Emily J. Dolbear, Melissa McDaniel, and Catherine Neitge
Photo Researcher: Svetlana Zhurkina
Photo Selector: Linda S. Koutris
Designer: The Design Lab
Cartographer: XNR Productions, Inc.

Library of Congress Cataloging-in-Publication Data
Burgan, Michael.
  Andrew Johnson / by Michael Burgan.
    p. cm. — (Profiles of the presidents)
Summary: A biography of the seventeenth president of the United States, from his humble beginnings
as a tailor in North Carolina through his controversial term as the first post-Civil War president and
beyond. Includes bibliographical references and index.
Contents: Rise and fall of a "common man"—Young tailor—New life in a new home—Rising political
star—On to Washington—Slavery divides the nation—Governor again—Freeing the slaves—From vice
president to president—Reconstruction—Battling the radicals—Fight in the cabinet—Impeachment—
Last days as president—New political efforts—The Senate–and the end.
  ISBN 0-7565-0264-0 (hardcover)
 1. Johnson, Andrew, 1808–1875—Juvenile literature. 2. Presidents—United States—Biography—
Juvenile literature. [1. Johnson, Andrew, 1808–1875. 2. Presidents.] I. Title. II. Series.
  E667 .B87 2003
  973.8'1'092—dc21   2002009942

Table of Contents

★ ★ ★

NOTE: In this book, words that are defined in the glossary are in **bold** *the first time they appear in the text.*

The Rise and Fall of a Common Man

★ ★ ★

On April 8, 1865, guns fell silent. After four bloody years, the Civil War was over. The North had defeated the South. The Union was saved and slavery ended. Just a few days later, however, another gun was fired. As

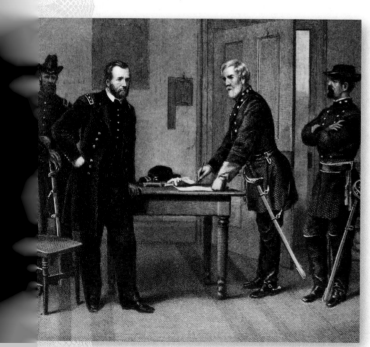

Confederate general Robert E. Lee (right) surrendering to Union general Ulysses S. Grant in Appomattox Court House, Virginia

President Abraham Lincoln enjoyed a play in Washington, D.C., John Wilkes Booth shot him. The president died the following day.

With Lincoln dead, the job of reconstructing the United States fell to Vice President Andrew Johnson. During the war, his home state of

Tennessee had voted to secede, or leave the Union. Tennessee had joined the Confederate States of America, a new country formed by Southern states that had seceded. Johnson, however, had remained loyal to the Union.

Johnson had grown up poor and never went to school. Through hard work, he built a business and educated himself. Johnson entered politics at an early age and became a talented speaker. He defended the interests of people like himself—workers, craftspeople, and farmers—who did not have much money or power. Johnson worked hard to support the common man. He enjoyed the challenge of a good political fight.

▼ A campaign poster from 1864 showing President Abraham Lincoln (left) and running mate Andrew Johnson

In many ways, Johnson's presidency turned into one long fight. He argued with Northerners in Congress who wanted to punish the South for leaving the Union. He also disagreed with them on how to treat the freedmen—the slaves who won their freedom after the Civil War (1861–1865). Johnson had owned slaves. He did not think free blacks should have the same rights as whites.

Johnson stood up for the rights of common people like these Tennessee settlers.

The 1868 impeachment trial of Andrew Johnson

Johnson's disagreements with Congress led to his breaking a law that he thought was wrong. The lawmakers took Johnson to court. The process of accusing an elected leader of a crime is called **impeachment.** Once accused, the leader must stand trial. Johnson was the first U.S. president to be impeached. The U.S. Senate found Johnson not guilty of the charges. Johnson's conflict with Congress, however, would dominate his presidency. His problems as president were part of the larger struggle to rebuild a nation torn apart by war and slavery.

◄ *A railroad depot that was destroyed by Union forces in Charleston, South Carolina*

The Young Tailor

★ ★ ★

Andrew Johnson was born on December 29, 1808, in Raleigh, North Carolina. His family lived in a small framed cabin. Johnson's father, Jacob, held a number of low-paying jobs. He died when Andrew was still quite young. Andrew's

The small framed ▶ cabin in Raleigh where Andrew Johnson was born

mother, Mary, supported him and his older brother, William, by making yarn and cloth. The family was poor. As an adult, Johnson said he had "grappled with the . . . monster called hunger." Even after his mother married her second husband, Turner Daugherty, the family struggled.

As a boy, Andrew did not go to school. Raleigh did not have public schools, and his mother could not afford to pay for private classes. The boy spent time playing with his brother and his cousins. When Andrew was nine, his mother arranged for him to work with a local tailor named James Selby. Andrew joined his brother at the shop. They were **apprentices,** which means they had to stay with Selby until they were twenty-one, work-ing for him as he taught them how to make clothes. Apprentices had little freedom and were not paid for their work, but most received an education. At Selby's shop, Andrew finally learned to read and write.

After almost two years at Selby's shop, Andrew and his

▼ Like the boys in this picture, Johnson and his brother were apprentices in a tailor's shop.

Eliza McCardle ▸
Johnson (above) and
Martha, one of the
five Johnson children

brother ran away. They had gotten into trouble in town and did not want to face Selby. They fled south, and Selby put out a reward for their capture. Andrew went to South Carolina, where he worked as a tailor for almost two years. He returned to Raleigh briefly in 1825, and then left for good the next year. Andrew, his mother, and stepfather went to Tennessee, where Andrew planned to open his own tailor shop.

Johnson settled in Greeneville, in eastern Tennessee. There, he met a young woman named Eliza McCardle. They were married in May 1826. Eliza was shy and did not like public gatherings. Through their long marriage, she remained in the background as Johnson became an important politician. Eliza raised their five children and supported Johnson through all his difficulties.

In Greeneville, the Johnsons rented a small, two-room house. They lived in back while Johnson did his tailoring in the front. Johnson was skillful with his needle and thread, and his business did well.

As Johnson worked, his wife sometimes read to him, and she helped him continue his education. Johnson

◄ *Johnson's tailor shop in Greeneville*

liked to read the speeches of historical figures. He soon had a chance to show off his own speaking skills. In 1828, Johnson entered a public **debate** over a new law passed in Tennessee. Johnson impressed the crowd with his arguments. He enjoyed the experience so much he joined a debating club at a local college.

War hero and ► seventh U.S. president Andrew Jackson

The next year, Tennesseeans celebrated when one of their own, Andrew Jackson, became the seventh president of the United States. Jackson was a former war hero. He defended the farmers and craftspeople of the South and the West. Jackson's supporters had formed the Democratic Party to combat the power of the wealthy.

A Rising Political Star

★ ★ ★

Jackson's success stirred Johnson and some of his friends to challenge the political leaders of Greeneville. Johnson was elected to the board of aldermen, the town's government. After being reelected a few times, Johnson became mayor of Greeneville in 1834.

◀ Johnson's home in Greeneville in the 1830s and 1840s

Johnson, once a poor, uneducated tailor, had become one of the leading citizens of the town. He walked the streets in fine clothes. He often stopped to talk about the issues of the day. Johnson decided that politics was his true calling. In 1835, he ran for a seat in the Tennessee **legislature,** which makes the laws for the state.

Johnson won the election. During his time in the state legislature, he usually voted against spending state money on new projects. He voted against building new railroads in eastern Tennessee—a project many people in the area supported. When Johnson ran again in 1837, Greeneville's leaders supported another **candidate,** and Johnson lost. He returned to tailoring, but two years later he ran a third time and won.

Over the next few years, Johnson traveled across Tennessee, working for the Democrats. The other major political party of the day was the Whigs. The Whigs favored a strong national government. The Democrats, including Johnson, wanted the states to have the freedom to do as they chose as much as possible.

Johnson debated Whigs and tried to strengthen the Democratic Party. His speeches sometimes attracted

The state capitol in Nashville

One of Johnson's ▶
political enemies,
William G. Brownlow

thousands of people. His forceful speaking style was developing. In his speeches, Johnson talked about the common man and his own simple roots. He also sometimes made personal attacks on the Whigs. One man said Johnson's speeches cut like a knife.

Johnson's style and beliefs appealed to many Tennesseans. In 1843, he was chosen to represent eastern Tennessee in the U.S. Congress. Of course, not everyone liked Johnson or his methods. A Whig newspaper editor, William G. Brownlow, called Johnson a "liar" and "low bred scoundrel." The two men remained political enemies for years.

In Washington, Johnson continued to support the poor and working people. He wanted Congress to pass his Homestead Act. This act would give 160 acres (65 hectares) of government land in the West to anyone who would settle on it and farm it for five years. The Homestead Act was not approved, but years later a law like it was passed. Johnson also supported laws that promoted the spread of slavery in new U.S. states and territories. Johnson did not like rich Southern slave owners, but he knew that many whites depended on slavery. By that time, he himself owned slaves.

Johnson sometimes fought with members of his own party. He took pride in his independent ways. Johnson once said, "I am no party man, bound by no party platform, and will vote as I please."

In 1852, Johnson returned to Tennessee to run for governor. Although some Democrats did not support him, Johnson won. As usual, Johnson appealed to workers and farmers. "They have so far never deserted me," he said after the election. "And God being willing, I will never desert them."

Andrew Johnson did ▶ not like wealthy Southerners who owned slaves, but he did favor slavery as an institution.

Preserving the Union

★   ★   ★

Johnson returned to Washington in December 1857 to serve in the U.S. Senate. By then, a new national party was replacing the Whigs. The Republican Party had been formed to oppose the spread of slavery in the United States.

▼ Johnson as a U.S. senator

The Republican Party was strongest in the North and West, while the Democratic Party was popular in the Southern states. In general, Democrats supported slavery and wanted to give new states the right to decide if they should allow it. Slavery was dividing the country in two.

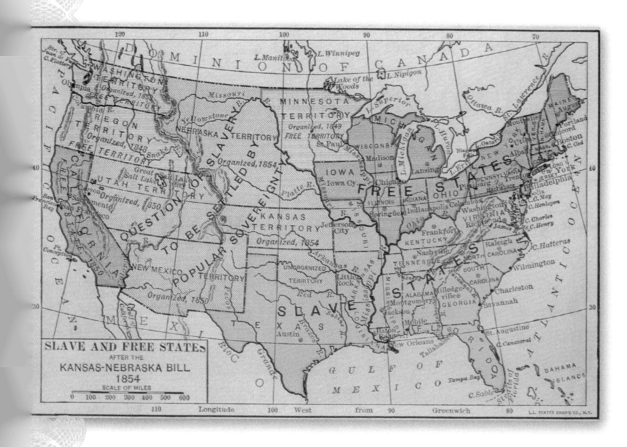

A map depicting the division of slave and free states in 1854

Johnson's position on slavery had not changed. He still welcomed it, though he did not always support the interests of wealthy slave owners. In the Senate, he said that Northerners had no right to try to end slavery in the South. Johnson, however, insisted the country should find a way to settle the conflict without breaking apart. The presidential election of 1860 would decide if the Union stayed together.

The Democrats chose Senator Stephen Douglas of Illinois to run against the Republican candidate, Abraham Lincoln, also of Illinois. Southerners in the Democratic Party then chose their own candidate, John C. Breckinridge. A fourth candidate, John Bell, also ran that year. Johnson supported Breckinridge, but Lincoln won the election.

◄ *Lincoln speaking during a debate with Douglas (in blue, seated behind Lincoln)*

Many Southerners were convinced that President Lincoln would end slavery. In December 1860, South Carolina voted to secede from the Union before this happened. Other Southern states soon followed. Johnson could not support dividing the country. He said in the Senate, "I am unwilling . . . to walk outside of the Union which has been the result of a **Constitution** made by the **patriots** of the Revolution." People in the North praised Johnson for this speech, but many Southerners saw him as a **traitor.** To Johnson, the traitors were the people who supported breaking up the Union.

After the Civil War began in April 1861, people in Tennessee were to vote on whether to secede from the

This Confederate banner illustrates the secession of the Southern states from the Union.

Union. On a trip home before the vote, Johnson faced angry crowds. At one point, he pulled out a gun to defend himself.

▲ As Civil War battles like this one began to occur, Tennesseans voted to secede.

In June, Tennessee voted to secede and join the Confederate States of America. Despite this vote, Johnson stayed in the U.S. Senate. He was the only senator from a Confederate state who did not resign, or quit. Johnson supported the Civil War because he believed that states

Union troops in ▶
Murfreesboro,
Tennessee, in 1862

had no right to secede. President Lincoln had the same
view. Neither man wanted to fight to end slavery. The war,
at least at first, was fought to keep the country whole.

By 1862, Union troops gained control of part of
Tennessee. In March, Lincoln named Johnson the state's
military governor. He ruled the state with complete power.

As governor, Johnson moved swiftly to crush support
for the Confederacy. He had the power to put people in
jail without trials, and he shut down newspapers that supported the South. Although he was tough at times,
Johnson also tried to be fair. Some former Confederates
who accepted his rule were released from jail.

As the Civil War dragged on, President Lincoln decided to free the slaves living in Confederate states. His **Emancipation Proclamation** of January 1863 freed the slaves in states that had seceded. The proclamation did not apply to slaves living in states that remained in the Union.

◄ *The Emancipation Proclamation freed slaves in the Confederate states.*

In Madison Co. Court!
LARGE SALE OF
LAND AND NEGROES

Petition for Sale of Land and Slaves.

Albert G. McClellan and others
vs.
Mary Vaden and husband, G. W. Vaden and others, distributees of Isabella McClellan, dec'd.

In the above cause, the undersigned, Clerk of the County Court of Madison county, Tenn., as commissioner, will expose to public sale on Saturday, 24th of March next, at the Court house, in the town of Jackson, that most desirable and conveniently situated Tract of Land, known as the McClellan farm, containing

1000 ACRES.

in one body, and lying within a mile and a half of the town of Jackson. Also, at the same time and place,

18 Or 20 NEGROES,

consisting of men, women and children. The land will be divided into tracts previous to the day of sale, and each division will be sold seperately.

Terms of sale.—Land on a credit of one and two years, and the negroes upon a credit of 12 months from the day of sale. Notes, with good security, will be required of purchasers, and lien retained on both land and negroes for the purchase money. Title to the land and negroes indisputable.

P. C. McCOWAT,
C. & M. Commissioner

Feb. 24, 1860.

A notice of a land ▶
and slave auction
in Tennessee

Johnson thought freeing the slaves in Tennessee would hurt the Union cause there. He wanted more time to win support from whites who owned slaves. Even though Tennessee had seceded, Johnson convinced Lincoln to treat the state as part of the Union. Lincoln agreed, and the Emancipation Proclamation did not free the slaves in Tennessee.

In October 1864, almost two years after Lincoln's proclamation, Johnson finally freed the slaves in his state. Though Johnson still believed in slavery, he knew it had to end for the Union to be strong. If slavery threatened the government, he said, "then the government has a clear right to destroy it."

President Lincoln was up for reelection in 1864. It would be a difficult race. The Republican Party and the Civil War were not popular. Lincoln wanted a Democrat who supported the Union to run with him. He thought this would help him win more votes. Lincoln picked Andrew Johnson as his vice presidential candidate.

Lincoln and Johnson won almost every state. On **Inauguration** Day, March 4, 1865, Johnson created quite a stir. Everyone could tell he was drunk. He had not been feeling well that morning, and he drank some whiskey to try to make himself feel better. His drunken speech seemed to confirm rumors that Johnson was an alcoholic. Most people who knew Johnson, however, said he was not a heavy drinker and never appeared drunk in public. The swearing-in speech was unusual. Still, some of Johnson's political enemies would continue to claim he was an alcoholic.

After winning the election, Lincoln and Johnson set about making plans on what to do when the Civil War ended. The North was about to win. Congress had passed an **amendment** to the Constitution ending slavery through-

The 1865 inauguration ▶
ceremony

out the country, and the states would eventually approve it. Lincoln wanted to bring the South back into the Union as peacefully as possible. The details of his plan are unknown, however, since he never had a chance to carry it out.

◄ Lincoln was shot at this theater in Washington, D.C. Secretary of State William Seward (below) was attacked in his home.

On the night of April 14, the president attended a play at Washington's Ford's Theatre. Johnson was home sleeping. At about 10 P.M., a neighbor woke Johnson to tell him the president had been shot. Secretary of State William Seward had been wounded in a separate attack at his home. Confederate supporters led by John Wilkes Booth had plotted the attacks. Johnson was also supposed to be shot, but his attacker had lost his nerve.

Johnson being sworn in as president after Lincoln's death

Johnson waited through the night to see if the president would survive. The next morning, Johnson learned that Lincoln was dead. Shortly after, he was sworn in as the seventeenth president of the United States.

Battling Congress

★ ★ ★

The period following the U.S. Civil War is called Reconstruction. During Reconstruction, the national government had to rebuild the Union as the South

◀ Government leaders during a Reconstruction meeting

United States, 1865
- States
- Territories
- Confederate States of America

rejoined the North. President Johnson took the lead during the first year of Reconstruction. In May 1865, he issued a rule allowing most Southerners to become U.S. citizens again if they swore loyalty to the Constitution. Confederate leaders were not allowed to take this loyalty oath. Johnson also forbade wealthy Southerners from taking the oath. The president, however, had the power to pardon people not allowed to take the oath.

Johnson did not give freed slaves the right to vote. Southern whites and some Northerners were glad Johnson denied blacks a role in the new Southern governments. However, many Northern Republicans in Congress were against this part of Johnson's Reconstruction plan.

Republicans controlled both the U.S. House of Representatives and the U.S. Senate. Some Republicans wanted to deal harshly with the former Confederates. They also wanted greater legal rights for freedmen. These Republicans were called Radical Republicans. At first, the Radical Republicans thought they could work with Johnson. One Radical Republican senator told the new president, "Johnson, we have faith in you. . . . There will be no trouble now running the government."

◀ Some whites were in favor of giving African-Americans like these North Carolina freedmen greater legal rights.

Thaddeus Stevens ▶
(above) and Charles
Sumner were Radical
Republican leaders.

Johnson and the Radical Republicans did not remain friendly for long. Johnson wanted to bring the South back into the Union as quickly and easily as possible. Many Republicans in Congress wanted to punish the Southern states. They also wanted to build their party's strength in the region.

Johnson pardoned more Confederate leaders than the Republicans wanted. This meant that the new state governments in the South were controlled by former Confederates. These state governments passed

The education of
freed blacks was one
of many issues that
divided Johnson and
the Radical
Republicans.

laws that denied blacks equal rights. The Republicans
soon realized Johnson was not as interested in helping
freedmen as they were. Johnson continued to believe the
state governments had the right to make their own deci-
sions, including how they treated freedmen.

Less than a year after becoming president, Johnson
was having serious trouble with Congress. In 1866,
Congress passed the Civil Rights Bill to protect the rights
of freedmen. Johnson vetoed, or rejected, the bill.

Celebration over the ▶
Civil Rights Bill
being passed

Congress approved the bill again, making it law anyway.
For the rest of his presidency, Johnson would battle
Congress over Reconstruction.

As Johnson struggled with the Radical Republicans, he
thought about forming a new party. He said, "We must res-
cue the power from their hands." Johnson hoped to unite
southern Democrats who supported the Union and northern Republicans who opposed the Radical Republicans.

In August 1866, Johnson toured the nation, speaking
out against the Radical Republicans who were running for

Congress. During several speeches, he argued with people in the audience. At one stop, a Johnson supporter yelled that some leading Republicans should be hanged. "Yes," Johnson agreed, "why not hang them." The speeches offended many Americans. The Radical Republicans now had even more reason to dislike Johnson.

Johnson became so unpopular that he could not even win praise for the good things that happened during his presidency. In 1867, his secretary of state, William

▼ *Andrew Johnson speaking from a train*

At the time, the purchase of Alaska was called "Seward's Folly."

Seward, bought Alaska from Russia for $7 million. At the time, some Americans thought the purchase was a waste of money. The deal was called "Seward's Folly." It took many years for Americans to realize it was a great bargain.

Meanwhile, relations between Johnson and Congress worsened. The Radicals and other Republicans worked together to pass Reconstruction laws that Johnson disliked. They also passed a law that affected how the president ran the government. The Tenure of Office Act of 1867 said Johnson could not remove members of his **cabinet** unless Congress agreed. Congress wanted to protect Secretary of War Edwin Stanton, who was a Radical Republican.

Johnson believed that Congress had no right to force him to keep cabinet members he did not want. He thought the Tenure of Office Act went against the Constitution, so Johnson fired Stanton. "If am to be impeached for this," Johnson said, "I am prepared."

◄ *Secretary of War Edwin Stanton*

Ulysses S. Grant defied the president.

Johnson named General Ulysses S. Grant to take Stanton's place. Despite Johnson's order, Stanton refused to leave his job. He believed Johnson was breaking the law. Grant also defied the president and did not take over for Stanton.

Some members of Congress had long wanted to impeach Johnson. The conflict over Stanton gave them even more reason. On February 24, 1868, the House of Representatives voted 126 to 47 that Johnson had committed "high crimes and misdemeanors." Their main charge was that he had disobeyed the Tenure of Office Act. After the vote, Johnson said, "Have I not been struggling . . . to uphold the Constitution which they are trampling under foot?"

After being impeached by the House, Johnson was tried in the Senate. Two-thirds of the senators had to agree for Johnson to be forced from office. That meant

◄ *Johnson (left) worked with a team of lawyers during the impeachment trial.*

that Johnson's enemies needed thirty-six votes. Yet for each of the three charges that the Senate voted on, the tally was 35–19. Johnson's presidency was saved by one vote.

After the trial, Johnson continued to fight with Congress. Despite everything, he still hoped to run for reelection in the fall of 1868. The Democrats, however, chose someone else as their candidate. The Democrats

United States, 1869
- States
- Territories

knew that Johnson was so hated by Northerners that he could not possibly win.

The Republican candidate, Ulysses S. Grant, won the election. He and Johnson had been enemies since the Stanton affair. Then, on the day Grant was sworn in, he insulted Johnson. Outgoing presidents usually rode to the inauguration with the new president, but Grant refused to ride with Johnson. The former president skipped the ceremony and spent the morning packing at the White House.

◀ *Johnson was not present at Grant's inauguration.*

The Former President

★ ★ ★

Back home in Greeneville, Tennessee, Johnson received a warmer welcome. Eight years before, some people in town had called him a traitor. Now, a banner hung across the street calling him a patriot.

DeWitt Senter ▾

Johnson did not want to leave politics. He wanted to show Americans that he had been right to challenge Congress. Johnson's goal was to return to Washington as a U.S. senator. He threw himself back into Tennessee politics. He worked to help elect a Republican named DeWitt Senter, who was running for governor. If Senter won the election, Johnson would have his support when he ran for the Senate.

Senter won the race. Johnson became a candidate for the Senate, but he still had too many enemies. For the first time since 1837, Johnson lost an election.

His next chance to return to Washington came in 1872, when he ran for the U.S. House of Representatives. The Democrats did not choose Johnson as their candidate, so he ran as an independent. The campaign was hard fought. The three candidates often debated each other. Johnson was a strong speaker, and he usually came out on top. Johnson lost the race, but he won new supporters.

▼ *Johnson survived a bout with cholera.*

In 1873, a deadly disease called cholera swept through Tennessee. Many people left the state. Johnson stayed in Greeneville to help his neighbors fight the disease. Then he caught it himself. He was sure he was going to die. Johnson wrote what he thought was his last letter, saying, "All seems gloom and despair." Johnson's health

U.S. SENATE

SPEECHES.

A. JOHNS. FROM TENN.

Political cartoonist
Thomas Nast drew
himself greeting
Andrew Johnson
when the former
president returned to
the Senate in 1875.
Nast had disagreed
with almost
everything Johnson
did while president.

improved, however. By the end of the year he was preparing for his next—and last—campaign.

The Tennessee legislature would choose the state's next U.S. senator. Johnson was one of six candidates. It took more than fifty tries before the lawmakers finally elected Johnson. After the last vote, a celebration broke out in the streets. During the celebration, Johnson gave another politician some advice. "Keep the common people on your side," he said, "and you will win."

Johnson's return to Washington was national news. He was the first, and still the only, former president to serve in the U.S. Senate. Johnson told a reporter, "I come sir, with the Constitution of my country in one hand, and the olive branch of peace in the other."

Some senators who had voted against Johnson during the impeachment trial were still in office. A few shook Johnson's hand. The rest ignored him. About three weeks

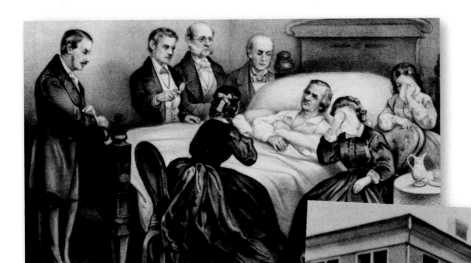

◀ *Johnson died only a few months after being elected to the Senate.*

▾ *Johnson's funeral in Greeneville*

later, Johnson made his first and only speech as a U.S. senator. He attacked President Grant for sending U.S. troops into Louisiana to defend its dishonest Republican governor. When he finished, Johnson said, "May God bless the country, and may God save the Constitution." Johnson was happy to be back in the Senate, making his views known.

A few months later, Johnson suffered a stroke while visiting his daughter Mary in Tennessee. He died on July 31, 1875. The former president was buried in Greeneville. His body was wrapped with an American flag, and a copy of the Constitution was placed beneath his head.

In the years after Johnson's death, most historians did not think highly of him. In later years, however, some historians called him brave for battling Congress over the Tenure of Office Act. Johnson had said the law went against the Constitution. Years later, the U.S. Supreme Court agreed. Still, Johnson had caused many of his own problems with his stubbornness and racism.

Andrew Johnson ▼ had a sometimes disagreeable relationship with Congress, but he still was a man of considerable political talent.

Johnson will always be remembered as the first U.S. president to be impeached. Just one vote kept him from being removed from office. His racist beliefs and his conflicts with Congress made Reconstruction a painful time for the United States.

Johnson had a rags-to-riches life. He worked hard to succeed and he had great political skills. He used those skills to support the Constitution and to restore the Union.

GLOSSARY

★ ★ ★

amendment—change

apprentices—people who work somewhere for free to learn a craft

cabinet—a president's group of advisers who are the heads of government departments

candidate—someone running for office in an election

constitution—a document stating the basic rules of a government

debate—a formal argument

Emancipation Proclamation—a document signed by President Abraham Lincoln during the Civil War, which freed the slaves in areas under Confederate control

impeachment—the process of charging an elected official with a serious crime

inauguration—a ceremony at which a president is sworn into office

legislature—the part of government that makes or changes laws

pardon—act that forgives a crime, so that the person who committed the crime is not punished

patriots—people who love their country

traitor—a person who betrays his or her country

vetoed—rejected

ANDREW JOHNSON'S LIFE AT A GLANCE

★ ★ ★

PERSONAL

Nickname:	None
Birth date:	December 29, 1808
Birthplace:	Raleigh, North Carolina
Father's name:	Jacob Johnson
Mother's name:	Mary McDonough Johnson
Education:	No formal education
Wife's name:	Eliza McCardle Johnson (1810–1876)
Married:	May 17, 1827
Children:	Martha Johnson (1828–1901); Charles Johnson (1830–1863); Mary Johnson (1832–1883); Robert Johnson (1834–1869); Andrew Johnson (1852–1879)
Died:	July 31, 1875, in Carter's Station, Tennessee
Buried:	Greeneville, Tennessee

PUBLIC

Occupation before presidency:	Tailor, public official
Occupation after presidency:	U.S. senator from Tennessee
Military service:	None
Other government positions:	Greeneville alderman; member of the Tennessee House of Representatives; Tennessee state senator; member of the U.S. House of Representatives from Tennessee; governor of Tennessee; U.S. senator from Tennessee; military governor of Tennessee; vice president
Political party:	Democrat
Vice president:	None
Dates in office:	April 15, 1865–March 3, 1869
Presidential opponent:	None
Number of votes (Electoral College):	None
Selected Writings:	*Papers of Andrew Johnson* (16 vols., 1967–2000)

Andrew Johnson's Cabinet

Secretary of state:
  William H. Seward (1865–1869)

Secretary of the treasury:
  Hugh McCulloch (1865–1869)

Secretary of war:
  Edwin M. Stanton (1865–1868)
  John M. Schofield (1868–1869)

Attorney general:
  James Speed (1865–1866)
  Henry Stanbery (1866–1868)
  William M. Evarts (1868–1869)

Postmaster general:
  William Dennison (1865–1866)
  Alexander W. Randall (1866–1869)

Secretary of the navy:
  Gideon Welles (1865–1869)

Secretary of the interior:
  John P. Usher (1865)
  James Harlan (1865–1866)
  Orville Browning (1866–1869)

ANDREW JOHNSON'S LIFE AND TIMES

★ ★ ★

JOHNSON'S LIFE		WORLD EVENTS

JOHNSON'S LIFE

December 29, Johnson is born in Raleigh, North Carolina — 1808

May 17, marries Eliza McCardle (above) — 1827

Elected an alderman of Greeneville, Tennessee — 1828

1810

1820

WORLD EVENTS

1810   Chile fights for its independence from Spain

1812–1814   The United States and Britain fight the War of 1812 (below)

1820   Susan B. Anthony (below), a leader of the American woman suffrage movement, is born

JOHNSON'S LIFE

WORLD EVENTS

Becomes mayor of
Greeneville — 1830

1830

1833   Great Britain
abolishes slavery

Joins the Tennessee
House of
Representatives (below) — 1835

1836   Texans defeat
Mexican
troops at San
Jacinto after a
deadly battle
at the Alamo
(right)

1837   American banker J. P.
Morgan is born

1840   1840   Auguste Rodin,
famous sculptor of
The Thinker (below),
is born in France

Becomes a member of
the U.S. House of
Representatives — 1843

JOHNSON'S LIFE

WORLD EVENTS

1848   *The Communist Manifesto,* by German writer Karl Marx, is widely distributed

1850

Becomes governor of 1853
Tennessee

1852   American Harriet Beecher Stowe (below) publishes *Uncle Tom's Cabin*

Elected to the 1857
U.S. Senate

1858   English scientist Charles Darwin (below) presents his theory of evolution

1860

President Abraham 1862
Lincoln appoints
Johnson military
governor of Tennessee

Elected vice
president under 1864
Abraham Lincoln

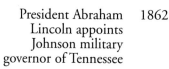

JOHNSON'S LIFE

WORLD EVENTS

1865 April 15, becomes president after Lincoln is killed

1865 *Tristan and Isolde,* by German composer Richard Wagner, opens in Munich

May 29, issues a rule allowing Southerners to regain their U.S. citizenship if they swear a loyalty oath to the Union

Lewis Carroll writes *Alice's Adventures in Wonderland*

1866 Congress passes the Civil Rights Act, overriding Johnson's veto

1866 The American Society for the Prevention of Cruelty to Animals is founded in New York City

1867 Congress passes the Tenure of Office Act, which prevents the president from firing members of his cabinet without Senate approval

1867 Laura Ingalls Wilder (below), author of the popular *Little House* books, is born

Secretary of State William Seward buys Alaska from Russia; the purchase is known as "Seward's Folly"

JOHNSON'S LIFE		WORLD EVENTS
February 24, the House of Representatives votes to impeach Johnson	1868	1868 · Louisa May Alcott publishes *Little Women*

March 13, impeachment trial in the Senate begins

May 16, acquitted by one vote in the Senate

December 25, grants a pardon to those Confederates who had not yet been given one

| Pardons three men who helped assassinate President Lincoln (below) | 1869 | 1869 · The transcontinental railroad across the United States (above) is completed |

The periodic table of elements is invented

Construction on the Brooklyn Bridge begins

The first Grand Central Station opens in New York City

JOHNSON'S LIFE			WORLD EVENTS
April 15, becomes president after Lincoln is killed	1865	1865	*Tristan and Isolde,* by German composer Richard Wagner, opens in Munich
May 29, issues a rule allowing Southerners to regain their U.S. citizenship if they swear a loyalty oath to the Union			Lewis Carroll writes *Alice's Adventures in Wonderland*

Congress passes the Civil Rights Act, overriding Johnson's veto	1866	1866	The American Society for the Prevention of Cruelty to Animals is founded in New York City
Congress passes the Tenure of Office Act, which prevents the president from firing members of his cabinet without Senate approval	1867	1867	Laura Ingalls Wilder (below), author of the popular *Little House* books, is born
Secretary of State William Seward buys Alaska from Russia; the purchase is known as "Seward's Folly"			

JOHNSON'S LIFE

1868

February 24, the House of Representatives votes to impeach Johnson

March 13, impeachment trial in the Senate begins

May 16, acquitted by one vote in the Senate

December 25, grants a pardon to those Confederates who had not yet been given one

1869

Pardons three men who helped assassinate President Lincoln (below)

WORLD EVENTS

1868

Louisa May Alcott publishes *Little Women*

1869

The transcontinental railroad across the United States (above) is completed

The periodic table of elements is invented

Construction on the Brooklyn Bridge begins

The first Grand Central Station opens in New York City

JOHNSON'S LIFE

WORLD EVENTS

1870

1870   John D. Rockefeller founds the Standard Oil Company

Elected to the   1875
U.S. Senate (above)

July 31, dies from
a stroke

1876   The Battle of the Little Bighorn is a victory for Native Americans defending their homes in the West against General George Custer (above)

Alexander Graham Bell uses the first telephone to speak to his assistant, Thomas Watson

UNDERSTANDING ANDREW JOHNSON AND HIS PRESIDENCY

★ ★ ★

IN THE LIBRARY

Dubowski, Cathy East. *Andrew Johnson: Rebuilding the Union.*
Englewood Cliffs, N.J.: Silver Burdett, 1991.

Harper, Judith E. *Andrew Johnson: Our Seventeenth President.*
Chanhassen, Minn.: The Child's World, 2002.

Malone, Mary. *Andrew Johnson.*
Berkeley Heights, N.J.: Enslow, 1999.

Morin, Isobel V. *Impeaching the President.*
Brookfield, Conn.: Millbrook Press, 1996.

Weber, Michael. *Civil War and Reconstruction.*
Austin, Tex.: Raintree/Steck-Vaughn, 2001.

ON THE WEB

The American President—Andrew Johnson
www.americanpresident.org/KoTRain/Courses/AJO/AJO_In_Brief.htm
To find out about Johnson's life and times

The Impeachment of Andrew Johnson
www.impeach-andrewjohnson.com
To learn more about Johnson's impeachment

Internet Public Library—Andrew Johnson
www.ipl.org/ref/POTUS/ajohnson.html
For information about Andrew Johnson's life and presidency

Reconstruction 1865–1880
www.ku.edu/history/VL/USA/ERAS/reconstruction.html
To learn about Reconstruction

JOHNSON HISTORIC SITES
ACROSS THE COUNTRY

Andrew Johnson National Historic Site
College and Depot Streets
P.O. Box 1088
Greeneville, TN 37744
423/638-3551
To visit Johnson's tailor shop and home
and the cemetery where he is buried

President Andrew Johnson Museum and Library
Tusculum College
Box 5026
Greeneville, TN 37743
423/638-4111
To see books and other artifacts belonging to Johnson

THE U.S. PRESIDENTS
(Years in Office)

★ ★ ★

1. **George Washington**
   (March 4, 1789-March 3, 1797)
2. **John Adams**
   (March 4, 1797-March 3, 1801)
3. **Thomas Jefferson**
   (March 4, 1801-March 3, 1809)
4. **James Madison**
   (March 4, 1809-March 3, 1817)
5. **James Monroe**
   (March 4, 1817-March 3, 1825)
6. **John Quincy Adams**
   (March 4, 1825-March 3, 1829)
7. **Andrew Jackson**
   (March 4, 1829-March 3, 1837)
8. **Martin Van Buren**
   (March 4, 1837-March 3, 1841)
9. **William Henry Harrison**
   (March 6, 1841-April 4, 1841)
10. **John Tyler**
    (April 6, 1841-March 3, 1845)
11. **James K. Polk**
    (March 4, 1845-March 3, 1849)
12. **Zachary Taylor**
    (March 5, 1849-July 9, 1850)
13. **Millard Fillmore**
    (July 10, 1850-March 3, 1853)
14. **Franklin Pierce**
    (March 4, 1853-March 3, 1857)
15. **James Buchanan**
    (March 4, 1857-March 3, 1861)
16. **Abraham Lincoln**
    (March 4, 1861-April 15, 1865)
17. **Andrew Johnson**
    (April 15, 1865-March 3, 1869)

18. **Ulysses S. Grant**
    (March 4, 1869-March 3, 1877)
19. **Rutherford B. Hayes**
    (March 4, 1877-March 3, 1881)
20. **James Garfield**
    (March 4, 1881-Sept 19, 1881)
21. **Chester Arthur**
    (Sept 20, 1881-March 3, 1885)
22. **Grover Cleveland**
    (March 4, 1885-March 3, 1889)
23. **Benjamin Harrison**
    (March 4, 1889-March 3, 1893)
24. **Grover Cleveland**
    (March 4, 1893-March 3, 1897)
25. **William McKinley**
    (March 4, 1897-
    September 14, 1901)
26. **Theodore Roosevelt**
    (September 14, 1901-
    March 3, 1909)
27. **William Howard Taft**
    (March 4, 1909-March 3, 1913)
28. **Woodrow Wilson**
    (March 4, 1913-March 3, 1921)
29. **Warren G. Harding**
    (March 4, 1921-August 2, 1923)
30. **Calvin Coolidge**
    (August 3, 1923-March 3, 1929)
31. **Herbert Hoover**
    (March 4, 1929-March 3, 1933)
32. **Franklin D. Roosevelt**
    (March 4, 1933-April 12, 1945)

33. **Harry S. Truman**
    (April 12, 1945-
    January 20, 1953)
34. **Dwight D. Eisenhower**
    (January 20, 1953-
    January 20, 1961)
35. **John F. Kennedy**
    (January 20, 1961-
    November 22, 1963)
36. **Lyndon B. Johnson**
    (November 22, 1963-
    January 20, 1969)
37. **Richard M. Nixon**
    (January 20, 1969-
    August 9, 1974)
38. **Gerald R. Ford**
    (August 9, 1974-
    January 20, 1977)
39. **James Earl Carter**
    (January 20, 1977-
    January 20, 1981)
40. **Ronald Reagan**
    (January 20, 1981-
    January 20, 1989)
41. **George H. W. Bush**
    (January 20, 1989-
    January 20, 1993)
42. **William Jefferson Clinton**
    (January 20, 1993-
    January 20, 2001)
43. **George W. Bush**
    (January 20, 2001-)

INDEX

★ ★ ★

ABOUT THE AUTHOR

Michael Burgan is a freelance writer of books for children and adults. A history graduate of the University of Connecticut, he has written more than thirty fiction and nonfiction children's books for various publishers. For adult audiences, he has written news articles, essays, and plays. Michael Burgan is a recipient of an Edpress Award and belongs to the Society of Children's Book Writers and Illustrators.